Fables for Our Time

BOOKS BY JAMES THURBER

Thurber & Company
Credo and Curios
Lantern and Lances
The Years with Ross
Alarms and Diversions
The Wonderful O
Further Fables for Our Time
Thurber's Dogs
Thurber Country
The Thurber Album
The 13 Clocks
The Beast in Me and Other Animals
The White Deer
The Thurber Carnival
The Great Quillow
Men, Women and Dogs
Many Moons
My World—and Welcome to It
Fables for Our Time
The Last Flower
Let Your Mind Alone
The Middle-Aged Man on the Flying Trapeze
My Life and Hard Times
The Seal in the Bedroom
The Owl in the Attic
Is Sex Necessary? (with E. B. White)

PLAY

The Male Animal (with Elliott Nugent)

REVUE

A Thurber Carnival

Fables for Our Time

and

Famous Poems
Illustrated

by

JAMES THURBER

PERENNIAL LIBRARY
Harper & Row, Publishers
New York, Evanston, San Francisco, London

FOR *HERMAN* AND *DOROTHY*

A hardcover edition of this book is available from Harper &
Row, Publishers.

FABLES FOR OUR TIME

Copyright, 1939, 1940, by James Thurber; copyright renewed
1968 by Helen Thurber. Printed in the United States of
America. All rights in this book are reserved. No part of the
book may be used or reproduced in any manner whatsoever
without written permission except in the case of brief quota-
tions embodied in critical articles and reviews. For information
address
Harper & Row, Publishers, Inc.
10 East 53d Street, New York, N.Y. 10022

First PERENNIAL LIBRARY edition published 1974.

STANDARD BOOK NUMBER: 06–080319–3

Contents

POEMS

Fables for Our Time

The Mouse Who Went
to the Country

ONCE upon a Sunday there was a city mouse who went to visit a country mouse. He hid away on a train the country mouse had told him to take, only to find that on Sundays it did not stop at Beddington. Hence the city mouse could not get off at Beddington and catch a bus for Sibert's Junction, where he was to be met by the country mouse. The city mouse, in fact, was carried on to Middleburg, where he waited three hours for a train to take him back. When he got back to Beddington he found that the last bus for Sibert's Junction had just left, so he ran and he ran and he ran and he finally caught the bus and crept aboard, only to find that it was not the bus for Sibert's Junction at all, but was going in the opposite direction through Pell's Hollow and Grumm to a place called Wimberby. When the bus finally stopped, the city mouse got out into a heavy rain and found that there were no more buses that night going anywhere. "To the hell with it," said the city mouse, and he walked back to the city.

Moral: Stay where you are, you're sitting pretty.

The Little Girl and the Wolf

ONE afternoon a big wolf waited in a dark forest for a little girl to come along carrying a basket of food to her grandmother. Finally a little girl did come along and she was carrying a basket of food. "Are you carrying that basket to your grandmother?" asked the wolf. The little girl said yes, she was. So the wolf asked her where her grandmother lived and the little girl told him and he disappeared into the wood.

When the little girl opened the door of her grandmother's house she saw that there was somebody in bed with a nightcap and nightgown on. She had approached no nearer than twenty-five feet from the bed when she saw that it was not her grandmother but the wolf, for even in a nightcap a wolf does not look any more like your grandmother than the Metro-Goldwyn lion looks like Calvin Coolidge. So the little girl took an automatic out of her basket and shot the wolf dead.

Moral: It is not so easy to fool little girls nowadays as it used to be.

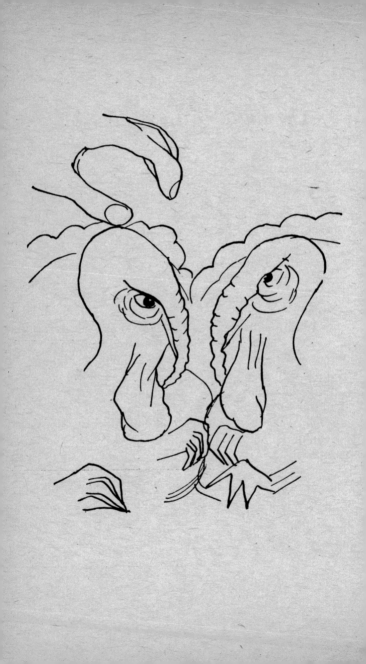

The Two Turkeys

ONCE upon a time there were two turkeys, an old turkey and a young turkey. The old turkey had been cock of the walk for many years and the young turkey wanted to take his place. "I'll knock that old buzzard cold one of these days," the young turkey told his friends. "Sure you will, Joe, sure you will," his friends said, for Joe was treating them to some corn he had found. Then the friends went and told the old turkey what the young turkey had said. "Why, I'll have his gizzard!" said the old turkey, setting out some corn for his visitors. "Sure you will, Doc, sure you will," said the visitors.

One day the young turkey walked over to where the old turkey was telling tales of his prowess in battle. "I'll bat your teeth into your crop," said the young turkey. "You and who else?" said the old turkey. So they began to circle around each other, sparring for an opening. Just then the farmer who owned the turkeys swept up the young one and carried him off and wrung his neck.

Moral: Youth will be served, frequently stuffed with chestnuts.

The Tiger
Who Understood People

ONCE upon a time there was a tiger who escaped from a zoo in the United States and made his way back to the jungle. During his captivity the tiger had learned a great deal about how men do things and he thought he would apply their methods to life in the jungle. The first day he was home he met a leopard and he said, "There's no use in you and me hunting for food; we'll make the other animals bring it to us." "How will we do that?" asked the leopard. "Easy," said the tiger, "you and I will tell everybody that we are going to put on a fight and that every animal will have to bring a freshly killed boar in order to get in and see the fight. Then we will just spar around and not hurt each other. Later you can say you broke a bone in your paw during the second round and I will say I broke a bone in my paw during the first round. Then we will announce a return engagement and they'll have to bring us more wild boars." "I don't think this will work," said the leopard. "Oh, yes it will," said the tiger. "You just go around saying that you can't help winning because I am a big palooka and I will go around saying I can't lose because you are a big palooka, and everybody will want to come and see the fight."

So the leopard went around telling everybody that he couldn't help winning because the tiger was a big palooka and the tiger went around telling everybody he couldn't lose because the leopard was a big palooka. The night of the fight came and the tiger and the leopard were very hungry because they hadn't gone out and done any hunting at all; they wanted to get the fight over as soon as possible and eat some of the freshly killed wild boars which all the animals would bring to the fight. But when the hour of the combat came none of the animals at all showed up. "The way I look at it," a fox had told them, "is this: if the leopard can't help winning and the tiger can't lose, it will be a draw and a draw is a very dull thing to watch, particularly when fought by fighters who are both big palookas." The animals all saw the logic of this and stayed away from the arena. When it got to be midnight and it was obvious that none of the animals would appear and that there wouldn't be any wild-boar meat to devour, the tiger and the leopard fell upon each other in a rage. The were both injured so badly and they were both so worn out by hunger that a couple of wild boars who came wandering along attacked them and killed them easily.

Moral: If you live as humans do, it will be the end of you.

The Fairly Intelligent Fly

A LARGE spider in an old house built a beautiful web in which to catch flies. Every time a fly landed on the web and was entangled in it the spider devoured him, so that when another fly came along he would think the web was a safe and quiet place in which to rest. One day a fairly intelligent fly buzzed around above the web so long without lighting that the spider appeared and said, "Come on down." But the fly was too clever for him and said, "I never light where I don't see other flies and I don't see any other flies in your house." So he flew away until he came to a place where there were a great many other flies. He was about to settle down among them when a bee buzzed up and said, "Hold it, stupid, that's flypaper. All those flies are trapped." "Don't be silly," said the fly, "they're dancing." So he settled down and became stuck to the flypaper with all the other flies.

Moral: There is no safety in numbers, or in anything else.

The Lion Who Wanted to Zoom

THERE was once a lion who coveted an eagle's wings. So he sent a message to the eagle asking him to call, and when the eagle came to the lion's den the lion said, "I will trade you my mane for your wings." "Keep talking, brother," said the eagle. "Without my wings I could no longer fly." "So what?" said the lion. "I can't fly now, but that doesn't keep me from being king of beasts. I became king of beasts on account of my magnificent mane." "All right," said the eagle, "but give me your mane first." "Just approach a little nearer," said the lion, "so that I can hand it to you." The eagle came closer and the lion clapped a huge paw on him, pinning him to the ground. "Come across with those wings!" he snarled.

So the lion took the eagle's wings but kept his own mane. The eagle was very despondent for a while and then he had an idea. "I bet you can't fly off the top of that great rock yonder," said the eagle. "Who, me?" said the lion, and he walked to the top of the rock and took off. His weight was too great for the eagle's wings to support, and besides he did not know how to fly, never having tried it before. So he crashed at the foot of the rock and burst into flames. The eagle hastily climbed down to him and regained his wings and took off the lion's mane, which he put about his own neck and shoulders. Flying back to the rocky nest where he lived with his mate, he decided to have some fun with her. So, covered with the lion's mane, he poked his head into the nest and in a deep, awful voice said *"Harrrooo!"* His mate, who was very nervous anyway, grabbed a pistol from a bureau drawer and shot him dead, thinking he was a lion.

Moral: Never allow a nervous female to have access to a pistol, no matter what you're wearing.

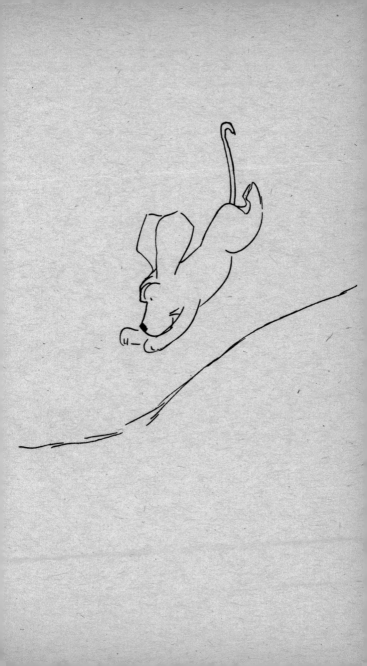

The Very Proper Gander

Not so very long ago there was a very fine gander. He was strong and smooth and beautiful and he spent most of his time singing to his wife and children. One day somebody who saw him strutting up and down in his yard and singing remarked, "There is a very proper gander." An old hen overheard this and told her husband about it that night in the roost. "They said something about propaganda," she said. "I have always suspected that," said the rooster, and he went around the barnyard next day telling everybody that the very fine gander was a dangerous bird, more than likely a hawk in gander's clothing. A small brown hen remembered a time when at a great distance she had seen the gander talking with some hawks in the forest. "They were up to no good," she said. A duck remembered that the gander had once told him he did not believe in anything. "He said to hell with the flag, too," said the duck. A guinea hen recalled that she had once seen somebody who looked very much like the gander throw something that looked a great deal like a bomb. Finally everybody snatched up sticks and stones and descended on the gander's house. He was strutting in his front yard, singing to his children and his wife. "There he is!" everybody cried. "Hawk-lover! Unbeliever! Flaghater! Bomb-thrower!" So they set upon him and drove him out of the country.

Moral: Anybody who you or your wife thinks is going to overthrow the government by violence must be driven out of the country.

The Moth and the Star

A YOUNG and impressionable moth once set his heart on a certain star. He told his mother about this and she counselled him to set his heart on a bridge lamp instead. "Stars aren't the thing to hang around," she said; "lamps are the thing to hang around." "You get somewhere that way," said the moth's father. "You don't get anywhere chasing stars," But the moth would not heed the words of either parent. Every evening at dusk when the star came out he would start flying toward it and every morning at dawn he would crawl back home worn out with his vain endeavor. One day his father said to him, "You haven't burned a wing in months, boy, and it looks to me as if you were never going to. All your brothers have been badly burned flying around street lamps and all your sisters have been terribly singed flying around house lamps. Come on, now, get out of here and get yourself scorched! A big strapping moth like you without a mark on him!"

The moth left his father's house, but he would not fly around street lamps and he would not fly around house lamps. He went right on trying to reach the star, which was four and one-third light years, or twenty-five trillion miles, away. The moth thought it was just caught in the top branches of an elm. He never did reach the star, but he went right on trying, night after night, and when he was a very, very old moth he began to think that he really had reached the star and he went around saying so. This gave him a deep and lasting pleasure, and he lived to a great old age. His parents and his brothers and his sisters had all been burned to death when they were quite young.

Moral: Who flies afar from the sphere of our sorrow is here today and here tomorrow.

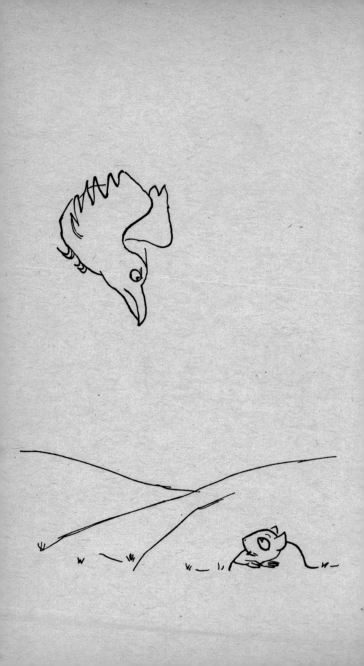

The Shrike and the Chipmunks

Once upon a time there were two chipmunks, a male and a female. The male chipmunk thought that arranging nuts in artistic patterns was more fun than just piling them up to see how many you could pile up. The female was all for piling up as many as you could. She told her husband that if he gave up making designs with the nuts there would be room in their large cave for a great many more and he would soon become the wealthiest chipmunk in the woods. But he would not let her interfere with his designs, so she flew into a rage and left him. "The shrike will get you," she said, "because you are helpless and cannot look after yourself." To be sure, the female chipmunk had not been gone three nights before the male had to dress for a banquet and could not find his studs or shirt or suspenders. So he couldn't go to the banquet, but that was just as well, because all the chipmunks who did go were attacked and killed by a weasel.

The next day the shrike began hanging around outside the chipmunk's cave, waiting to catch him. The shrike couldn't get in because the doorway was clogged up with soiled laundry and dirty dishes. "He will come out for a walk after breakfast and I will get him then," thought the shrike. But the chipmunk slept all day and did not get up and have breakfast until after dark. Then he came out for a breath of air before beginning work on a new design. The shrike swooped down to snatch up the chipmunk, but could not see very well on account of the dark, so he batted his head against an alder branch and was killed.

A few days later the female chipmunk returned and saw the awful mess the house was in. She went to the bed and shook her husband. "What would you do without me?" she demanded. "Just go on living, I guess," he said. "You wouldn't last five days," she told him. She swept the house and did the dishes and sent out the laundry, and then she made the chipmunk get up and wash and dress. "You can't be healthy if you lie in bed all day and never get any exercise," she told him. So she took him for a walk in the bright sunlight and they were both caught and killed by the shrike's brother, a shrike named Stoop.

Moral: Early to rise and early to bed makes a male healthy and wealthy and dead.

The Seal Who Became Famous

A SEAL who lay basking on a large, smooth rock said
to himself: all I ever do is swim. None of the
other seals can swim any better than I can, he re-
flected, but, on the other hand, they can all swim just
as well. The more he pondered the monotony and
uniformity of his life, the more depressed he became.
That night he swam away and joined a circus.

Within two years the seal had become a great
balancer. He could balance lamps, billiard cues, medicine balls, hassocks, taborets, dollar cigars, and anything else you gave him. When he read in a book a
reference to the Great Seal of the United States, he
thought it meant him. In the winter of his third year
as a performer he went back to the large, smooth rock
to visit his friends and family. He gave them the Big
Town stuff right away: the latest slang, liquor in a
golden flask, zippers, a gardenia in his lapel. He
balanced for them everything there was on the rock
to balance, which wasn't much. When he had run
through his repertory, he asked the other seals if they
could do what he had done and they all said no.
"O. K.," he said. "Let's see you do something I can't
do." Since the only thing they could do was swim,
they all plunged off the rock into the sea. The circus
seal plunged right after them, but he was so hampered

by his smart city clothes, including a pair of seventeen-dollar shoes, that he began to founder at once. Since he hadn't been in swimming for three years, he had forgot what to do with his flippers and tail, and he went down for the third time before the other seals could reach him. They gave him a simple but dignified funeral.

Moral: Whom God has equipped with flippers should not monkey around with zippers.

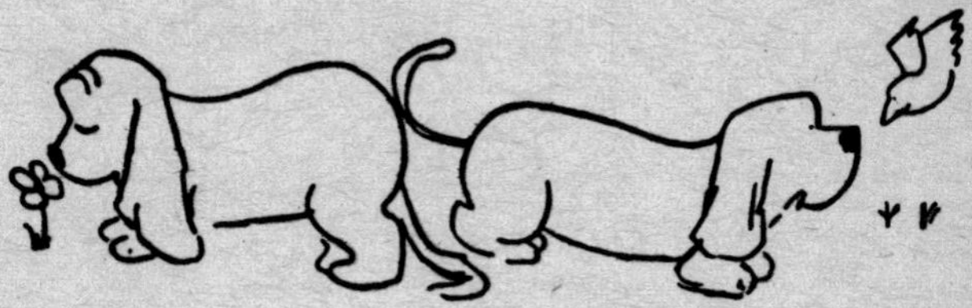

The Hunter and the Elephant

ONCE upon a time there was a hunter who spent the best years of his life looking for a pink elephant. He looked in Cathay and he looked in Africa; he looked in Zanzibar and he looked in India; but he couldn't find one. The longer he looked, the more he wanted a pink elephant. He would trample black orchids and he would walk right past purple cows, so intent was he on his quest. Then one day in a far corner of the world he came upon a pink elephant and he spent ten days digging a trap for it and he hired forty natives to help him drive the elephant into the trap. The pink elephant was finally captured and tied up and taken back to America.

When the hunter got home, he found that his farm was really no place for an elephant. It trampled his wife's dahlias and peonies, it broke his children's toys, it crushed the smaller animals around the place, and it smashed pianos and kitchen cabinets as if they were berry boxes. One day, when the hunter had had the elephant for about two years, he woke up to find that his wife had left his bed and his children had left his board and all the animals on the estate were dead except the elephant. The elephant was the same as ever except that it had faded. It wasn't pink any more. It was white.

Moral: A burden in the bush is worth two on your hands.

The Scotty Who
Knew Too Much

SEVERAL summers ago there was a Scotty who went to the country for a visit. He decided that all the farm dogs were cowards, because they were afraid of a certain animal that had a white stripe down its back. "You are a pussy-cat and I can lick you," the Scotty said to the farm dog who lived in the house where the Scotty was visiting. "I can lick the little animal with the white stripe, too. Show him to me." "Don't you want to ask any questions about him?" said the farm dog. "Naw," said the Scotty. "*You* ask the questions."

So the farm dog took the Scotty into the woods and showed him the white-striped animal and the Scotty closed in on him, growling and slashing. It was all over in a moment and the Scotty lay on his back. When he came to, the farm dog said, "What happened?" "He threw vitriol," said the Scotty, "but he never laid a glove on me."

A few days later the farm dog told the Scotty there was another animal all the farm dogs were afraid of. "Lead me to him," said the Scotty. "I can lick anything that doesn't wear horseshoes." "Don't you want to ask any questions about him?" said the farm dog.

"Naw," said the Scotty, "Just show me where he hangs out." So the farm dog led him to a place in the woods and pointed out the little animal when he came along. "A clown," said the Scotty, "a pushover," and he closed in, leading with his left and exhibiting some mighty fancy footwork. In less than a second the Scotty was flat on his back, and when he woke up the farm dog was pulling quills out of him. "What happened?" said the farm dog. "He pulled a knife on me," said the Scotty, "but at least I have learned how you fight out here in the country, and now I am going to beat *you* up." So he closed in on the farm dog, holding his nose with one front paw to ward off the vitriol and covering his eyes with the other front paw to keep out the knives. The Scotty couldn't see his opponent and he couldn't smell his opponent and he was so badly beaten that he had to be taken back to the city and put in a nursing home.

Moral: It is better to ask some of the questions than to know all the answers.

The Bear Who Let It Alone

IN THE woods of the Far West there once lived a brown bear who could take it or let it alone. He would go into a bar where they sold mead, a fermented drink made of honey, and he would have just two drinks. Then he would put some money on the bar and say, "See what the bears in the back room will have," and he would go home. But finally he took to drinking by himself most of the day. He would reel home at night, kick over the umbrella stand, knock down the bridge lamps, and ram his elbows through the windows. Then he would collapse on the floor and lie there until he went to sleep. His wife was greatly distressed and his children were very frightened.

At length the bear saw the error of his ways and began to reform. In the end he became a famous teetotaller and a persistent temperance lecturer. He would tell everybody that came to his house about the awful effects of drink, and he would boast about how strong and well he had become since he gave up touching the stuff. To demonstrate this, he would stand on his head and on his hands and he would turn cartwheels in the house, kicking over the umbrella stand, knocking down the bridge lamps, and ramming his elbows through the windows. Then he would lie down on the floor, tired by his healthful exercise, and go to sleep. His wife was greatly distressed and his children were very frightened.

Moral: You might as well fall flat on your face as lean over too far backward.

The Owl Who Was God

O NCE upon a starless midnight there was an owl who sat on the branch of an oak tree. Two ground moles tried to slip quietly by, unnoticed. "You!" said the owl. "Who?" they quavered, in fear and astonishment, for they could not believe it was possible for anyone to see them in that thick darkness. "You two!" said the owl. The moles hurried away and told the other creatures of the field and forest that the owl was the greatest and wisest of all animals because he could see in the dark and because he could answer any question. "I'll see about that," said a secretary bird, and he called on the owl one night when it was again very dark. "How many claws am I holding up?" said the secretary bird. "Two," said the owl, and that was right. "Can you give me another expression for 'that is to say' or 'namely'?" asked the secretary bird. "To wit," said the owl. "Why does a lover call on his love?" asked the secretary bird. "To woo," said the owl.

The secretary bird hastened back to the other creatures and reported that the owl was indeed the greatest and wisest animal in the world because he could see in the dark and because he could answer any question. "Can he see in the daytime, too?" asked a red fox. "Yes," echoed a dormouse and a French poodle. "Can he see in the daytime, too?" All the other creatures laughed loudly at this silly question, and they set upon the red fox and his friends and drove them out of the region. Then they sent a messenger to the owl and asked him to be their leader.

When the owl appeared among the animals it was high noon and the sun was shining brightly. He walked very slowly, which gave him an appearance of great dignity, and he peered about him with large, staring eyes, which gave him an air of tremendous importance. "He's God!" screamed a Plymouth Rock hen. And the others took up the cry "He's God!" So they followed him wherever he went and when he began to bump into things they began to bump into things, too. Finally he came to a concrete highway and he started up the middle of it and all the other creatures followed him. Presently a hawk, who was acting as outrider, observed a truck coming toward them at fifty miles an hour, and he reported to the secretary bird and the secretary bird reported to the owl. "There's danger ahead," said the secretary bird. "To wit?" said the owl. The secretary bird told him. "Aren't you afraid?" he asked. "Who?" said the owl calmly, for he could not see the truck. "He's God!" cried all the creatures again, and they were still crying "He's God!" when the truck hit them and ran them down. Some of the animals were merely injured, but most of them, including the owl, were killed.

Moral: You can fool too many of the people too much of the time.

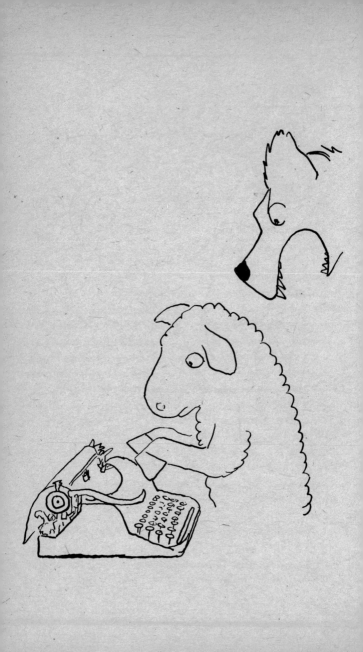

The Sheep in Wolf's Clothing

Not very long ago there were two sheep who put on wolf's clothing and went among the wolves as spies, to see what was going on. They arrived on a fete day, when all the wolves were singing in the taverns or dancing in the street. The first sheep said to his companion, "Wolves are just like us, for they gambol and frisk. Every day is fete day in Wolfland." He made some notes on a piece of paper (which a spy should never do) and he headed them "My Twenty-Four Hours in Wolfland," for he had decided not to be a spy any longer but to write a book on Wolfland and also some articles for the *Sheep's Home Companion*. The other sheep guessed what he was planning to do, so he slipped away and began to write a book called "My Ten Hours in Wolfland." The first sheep suspected what was up when he found his friend had gone, so he wired a book to his publisher called "My Five Hours in Wolfland," and it was announced for publication first. The other sheep immediately sold his manuscript to a newspaper syndicate for serialization.

Both sheep gave the same message to their fellows: wolves were just like sheep, for they gambolled and frisked, and every day was fete day in Wolfland. The citizens of Sheepland were convinced by all this, so they drew in their sentinels and they let down their barriers. When the wolves descended on them one night, howling and slavering, the sheep were as easy to kill as flies on a windowpane.

Moral: Don't get it right, just get it written.

The Stork Who Married
a Dumb Wife

A DANISH stork was in the habit of spending six
nights a week out on the town with the boys,
drinking and dicing and playing the match game.
His wife had never left their nest, which was on a
chimney top, since he married her, for he did not
want her to get wise to the ways of the male. When
he got home, which was usually at four o'clock in the
morning—unless the party had gone on to Reuben's—
he always brought her a box of candy and handed
it to her together with a stork story, which is the
same as a cock-and-bull story. "I've been out deliver-
ing babies," he would say. "It's killing me, but it is
my duty to go on." "Who do you deliver babies for?"
she asked one morning. "Human beings," he said.
"A human being cannot have a baby without help
from someone. All the other animals can, but human
beings are helpless. They depend on the other animals for everything from food and clothing to com-
panionship." Just then the phone rang and the stork
answered it. "Another baby on the way," he said
when he had hung up. "I'll have to go out again to-
night." So that night he went out again and did not
get home until seven-thirty in the morning. "Thish

was very special case," he said, handing his wife a box of candy. "Five girls." He did not add that the five girls were all blondes in their twenties.

After a while the female stork got to thinking. Her husband had told her never to leave the nest, because the world was full of stork traps, but she began to doubt this. So she flew out into the world, looking and listening. In this way she learned to tell time and to take male talk with a grain of salt; she found out that candy is dandy, as the poet has said, but that licker is quicker; she discovered that the offspring of the human species are never brought into the world by storks. This last discovery was a great blow to her, but it was a greater blow to Papa when he came home the next morning at a quarter to six. "Hello, you phony obstetrician," said his wife coldly. "How are all the blonde quintuplets today?" And she crowned him with a chimney brick.

Moral: The male was made to lie and roam, but woman's place is in the home.

The Green Isle in the Sea

ONE sweet morning in the Year of Our Lord, Nineteen hundred and thirty-nine, a little old gentleman got up and threw wide the windows of his bedroom, letting in the living sun. A black widow spider, who had been dozing on the balcony, slashed at him, and although she missed, she did not miss very far. The old gentleman went downstairs to the dining-room and was just sitting down to a splendid breakfast when his grandson, a boy named Burt, pulled the chair from under him. The old man's hip was strained but it was fortunately not broken.

Out in the street, as he limped toward a little park with many trees, which was to him a green isle in the sea, the old man was tripped up by a gaily colored hoop sent rolling at him, with a kind of disinterested deliberation, by a grim little girl. Hobbling on a block farther, the old man was startled, but not exactly surprised, when a bold daylight robber stuck a gun in his ribs. "Put 'em up, Mac," said the robber, "and come across." Mac put them up and came across with his watch and money and a gold ring his mother had given him when he was a boy.

When at last the old gentleman staggered into the little park, which had been to him a fountain and a shrine, he saw that half the trees had been killed by a blight, and the other half by a bug. Their leaves were gone and they no longer afforded any protection from the skies, so that the hundred planes which appeared suddenly overhead had an excellent view of the little old gentleman through their bombing-sights.

Moral: The world is so full of a number of things, I am sure we should all be as happy as kings, and you know how happy kings are.

The Crow and the Oriole

ONCE upon a time a crow fell in love with a Baltimore oriole. He had seen her flying past his nest every spring on her way North and every autumn on her way South, and he had decided that she was a tasty dish. He had observed that she came North every year with a different gentleman, but he paid no attention to the fact that all the gentlemen were Baltimore orioles. "Anybody can have that mouse," he said to himself. So he went to his wife and told her that he was in love with a Baltimore oriole who was as cute as a cuff link. He said he wanted a divorce, so his wife gave him one simply by opening the door and handing him his hat. "Don't come crying to me when she throws you down," she said. "That fly-by-season hasn't got a brain in her head. She can't cook or sew. Her upper register sounds like a streetcar taking a curve. You can find out in any dictionary that the crow is the smartest and most capable of birds—or was till you became one." "Tush!" said the male crow. "Pish! You are simply a jealous woman." He tossed her a few dollars. "Here," he said, "go buy yourself some finery. You look like the bottom of an old teakettle." And off he went to look for the oriole.

This was in the springtime and he met her coming North with an oriole he had never seen before. The crow stopped the female oriole and pleaded his cause —or should we say cawed his pleas? At any rate, he courted her in a harsh, grating voice, which made her laugh merrily. "You sound like an old window shutter," she said, and she snapped her fingers at him. "I am bigger and stronger than your gentleman friend," said the crow. "I have a vocabulary larger than his. All the orioles in the country couldn't even lift the corn I own. I am a fine sentinel and my voice can be heard for miles in case of danger." "I don't see how that could interest anybody but another crow," said the female oriole, and she laughed at him and flew on toward the North. The male oriole tossed the crow some coins. "Here," he said, "go buy yourself a blazer or something. You look like the bottom of an old coffeepot."

The crow flew back sadly to his nest, but his wife was not there. He found a note pinned to the front door. "I have gone away with Bert," it read. "You will find some arsenic in the medicine chest."

Moral: Even the llama should stick to mamma.

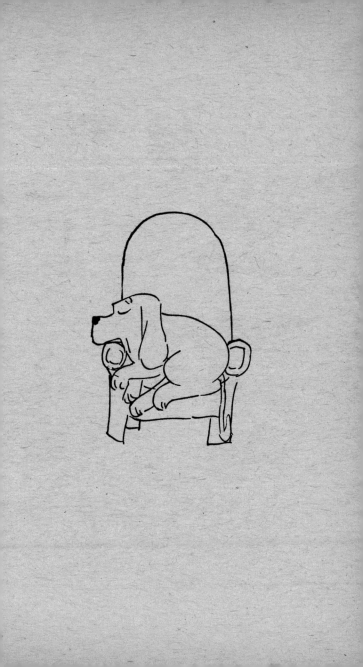

The Elephant Who
Challenged the World

A<small>N</small> ELEPHANT who lived in Africa woke up one
morning with the conviction that he could de-
feat all the other animals in the world in single combat, one at a time. He wondered that he hadn't
thought of it before. After breakfast he called first on
the lion. "You are only the King of Beasts," bellowed
the elephant, "whereas I am the Ace!" and he demon-
strated his prowess by knocking the lion out in fifteen
minutes, no holds barred. Then in quick succession
he took on the wild boar, the water buffalo, the
rhinoceros, the hippopotamus, the giraffe, the zebra,
the eagle, and the vulture, and he conquered them
all. After that the elephant spent most of his time in
bed eating peanuts, while the other animals, who
were now his slaves, built for him the largest house
any animal in the world had ever had. It was five
stories high, solidly made of the hardest woods to be
found in Africa. When it was finished, the Ace of
Beasts moved in and announced that he could pin
back the ears of any animal in the world. He challenged all comers to meet him in the basement of the
big house, where he had set up a prize ring ten times
the regulation size.

Several days went by and then the elephant got an anonymous letter accepting his challenge. "Be in your basement tomorrow afternoon at three o'clock," the message read. So at three o'clock the next day the elephant went down to the basement to meet his mysterious opponent, but there was no one there, or at least no one he could see. "Come out from behind whatever you're behind!" roared the elephant. "I'm not behind anything," said a tiny voice. The elephant tore around the basement, upsetting barrels and boxes, banging his head against the furnace pipes, rocking the house on its foundations, but he could not find his opponent. At the end of an hour the elephant roared that the whole business was a trick and a deceit—probably ventriloquism—and that he would never come down to the basement again. "Oh, yes you will," said the tiny voice. "You will be down here at three o'clock tomorrow and you'll end up on your back." The elephant's laughter shook the house. "We'll see about that," he said.

The next afternoon the elephant, who slept on the fifth floor of the house, woke up at two-thirty o'clock and looked at his wristwatch. "Nobody I can't see will ever get me down to the basement again," he growled, and went back to sleep. At exactly three o'clock the house began to tremble and quiver as if an earthquake had it in its paws. Pillars and beams bent and broke like reeds, for they were all drilled full of tiny holes. The fifth floor gave way completely and crashed down upon the fourth, which fell upon the third, which fell upon the second, which carried away the first as if it had been the floor of a berry basket. The elephant was precipitated into the basement, where he fell heavily upon the concrete floor and lay there on his back, completely unconscious. A tiny voice began to count him out. At the count of ten the elephant came to, but he could not get up. "What animal are you?" he demanded of the mysterious voice in a quavering tone which had lost its menace. "I am the termite," answered the voice.

The other animals, straining and struggling for a week, finally got the elephant lifted out of the basement and put him in jail. He spent the rest of his life there, broken in spirit and back.

Moral: The battle is sometimes to the small, for the bigger they are the harder they fall.

The Birds and the Foxes

ONCE upon a time there was a bird sanctuary in which hundreds of Baltimore orioles lived together happily. The refuge consisted of a forest entirely surrounded by a high wire fence. When it was put up, a pack of foxes who lived nearby protested that it was an arbitrary and unnatural boundary. However, they did nothing about it at the time because they were interested in civilizing the geese and ducks on the neighboring farms. When all the geese and ducks had been civilized, and there was nothing else left to eat, the foxes once more turned their attention to the bird sanctuary. Their leader announced that there had once been foxes in the sanctuary but that they had been driven out. He proclaimed that Baltimore orioles belonged in Baltimore. He said, furthermore, that the orioles in the sanctuary were a continuous menace to the peace of the world. The other animals cautioned the foxes not to disturb the birds in their sanctuary.

So the foxes attacked the sanctuary one night and tore down the fence that surrounded it. The orioles rushed out and were instantly killed and eaten by the foxes.

The next day the leader of the foxes, a fox from whom God was receiving daily guidance, got upon the rostrum and addressed the other foxes. His message was simple and sublime. "You see before you," he said, "another Lincoln. We have liberated all those birds!"

Moral: Government of the orioles, by the foxes, and for the foxes, must perish from the earth.

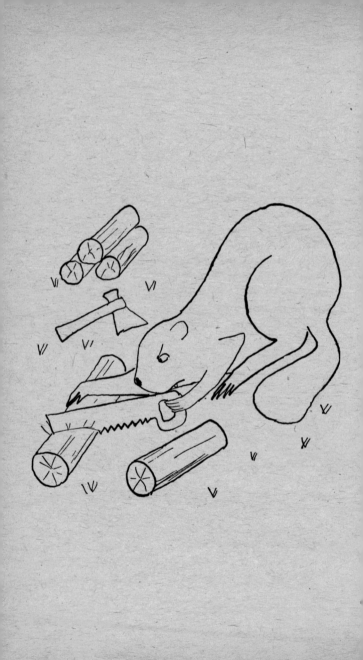

The Courtship of Arthur and Al

O NCE upon a time there was a young beaver named Al and an older beaver named Arthur. They were both in love with a pretty little female. She looked with disfavor upon the young beaver's suit because he was a harum-scarum and a ne'er-do-well. He had never done a single gnaw of work in his life, for he preferred to eat and sleep and to swim lazily in the streams and to play Now-I'll-Chase-You with the girls. The older beaver had never done anything but work from the time he got his first teeth. He had never played anything with anybody.

When the young beaver asked the female to marry him, she said she wouldn't think of it unless he amounted to something. She reminded him that Arthur had built thirty-two dams and was working on three others, whereas he, Al, had never even made a bread-board or a pin tray in his life. Al was very sorry, but he said he would never go to work just because a woman wanted him to. Thereupon she offered to be a sister to him, but he pointed out that he already had seventeen sisters. So he went back to eating and sleeping and swimming in the streams and playing Spider-in-the-Parlor with the girls. The female married Arthur one day at the lunch hour—he could never get away from work for more than one hour at a time. They had seven children and Arthur worked so hard supporting them he wore his teeth down to the gum line. His health broke in two before long and he died without ever having had a vacation in his life. The young beaver continued to eat and sleep and swim in the streams and play Unbutton-Your-Shoe with the girls. He never Got Anywhere, but he had a long life and a Wonderful Time.

Moral: It is better to have loafed and lost than never to have loafed at all.

The Hen Who Wouldn't Fly

IN ONE of the Midwestern states there lived a speck-led hen who was opposed to aviation. In her youth, watching a flight of wild geese going north, she had seen two fall (shot by hunters), go into a nose dive, and crash into the woods. So she went about the countryside saying that flying was very dangerous and that any fowl with any sense would stick to the solid earth. Every time she had to cross a concrete highway near her farm she ran on foot, screaming and squawk-ing; sometimes she made it easily, at other times she was almost tagged by passing cars. Five of her sisters and three of her daughters' husbands were killed trying to cross the road in one month (July).

Before long an enterprising wood duck set up an airways service across the road and back. He charged five grains of corn to take a hen or a rooster across, two grains for a chick. But the speckled hen, who was a power in the community, went around clucking and cut-cutting and cadawcutting and telling every-body that air travel was not safe and never would be. She persuaded the chickens not to ride on the duck's back, and he failed in business and returned to the forests. Before the year was out, the speckled hen, four more of her sisters, three of her sons-in-law, four aunts, and a grandfather had been killed trying to cross the road on foot.

Moral: Use the wings God gave you, or nothing can save you.

The Glass in the Field

A SHORT time ago some builders, working on a studio in Connecticut, left a huge square of plate glass standing upright in a field one day. A goldfinch flying swiftly across the field struck the glass and was knocked cold. When he came to he hastened to his club, where an attendant bandaged his head and gave him a stiff drink. "What the hell happened?" asked a sea gull. "I was flying across a meadow when all of a sudden the air crystallized on me," said the goldfinch. The sea gull and a hawk and an eagle all laughed heartily. A swallow listened gravely. "For fifteen years, fledgling and bird, I've flown this country," said the eagle, "and I assure you there is no such thing as air crystallizing. Water, yes; air, no." "You were probably struck by a hailstone," the hawk told the goldfinch. "Or he may have had a stroke," said the sea gull. "What do you think, swallow?" "Why, I—I think maybe the air crystallized on him," said the swallow. The large birds laughed so loudly that the goldfinch became annoyed and bet them each a dozen worms that they couldn't follow the course he had flown across the field without encountering the hardened atmosphere. They all took his bet; the swallow went along to watch. The sea gull, the eagle, and the hawk decided to fly together over the route the goldfinch indicated. "You come, too," they said to the swallow. "I—I—well, no," said the swallow. "I don't think I will." So the three large birds took off together and they hit the glass together and they were all knocked cold.

Moral: *He who hesitates is sometimes saved.*

The Tortoise and the Hare

THERE was once a wise young tortoise who read in an ancient book about a tortoise who had beaten a hare in a race. He read all the other books he could find but in none of them was there any record of a hare who had beaten a tortoise. The wise young tortoise came to the natural conclusion that he could outrun a hare, so he set forth in search of one. In his wanderings he met many animals who were willing to race him: weasels, stoats, dachshunds, badger-boars, short-tailed field mice, and ground squirrels. But when the tortoise asked if they could outrun a hare, they all said no, they couldn't (with the exception of a dachshund named Freddie, and nobody paid any attention to him). "Well, I can," said the tortoise, "so there's no use wasting my time on you." And he continued his search.

After many days, the tortoise finally encountered a hare and challenged him to a race. "What are you going to use for legs?" asked the hare. "Never mind that," said the tortoise. "Read this." He showed the hare the story in the ancient book, complete with moral about the swift not always being so terribly fast. "Tosh," said the hare. "You couldn't go fifty feet in an hour and a half, whereas I can go fifty feet in one and a fifth seconds." "Posh," said the tortoise.

"You probably won't even finish second." "We'll see about that," said the hare. So they marked off a course fifty feet long. All the other animals gathered around. A bullfrog set them on their marks, a gun dog fired a pistol, and they were off.

When the hare crossed the finish line, the tortoise had gone approximately eight and three-quarter inches.

Moral: A new broom may sweep clean, but never trust an old saw.

The Patient Bloodhound

IN MAY, 1937, a bloodhound who lived in Wapokoneta Falls, Ohio, was put on the trail of a man
suspected of a certain crime. The bloodhound followed him to Akron, Cleveland, Buffalo, Syracuse,
Rochester, Albany, and New York. The Westminster
dog show was going on at the time but the bloodhound couldn't get to the garden because the man got
on the first ship for Europe. The ship landed at Cher-
bourg and the bloodhound followed the man to Paris,
Beauvais, Calais, Dover, London, Chester, Llandudno,
Bettws-y-Coed, and Edinburgh, where the dog wasn't
able to take in the international sheep trials. From
Edinburgh, the bloodhound trailed the man to Liverpool, but since the man immediately got on a ship for
New York, the dog didn't have a chance to explore
the wonderful Liverpool smells.

In America again, the bloodhound traced the man
to Teaneck, Tenafly, Nyack, and Peapack—where the
dog didn't have time to run with the Peapack beagles.
From Peapack the hound followed the man to Cincinnati, St. Louis, Kansas City, St. Louis, Cincinnati,
Columbus, Akron, and finally back to Wapokoneta
Falls. There the man was acquitted of the crime he
had been followed for.

The bloodhound had developed fallen paw-pads

and he was so worn out he could never again trail anything that was faster than a turtle. Furthermore, since he had gone through the world with his eyes and nose to the ground, he had missed all its beauty and excitement.

Moral: The paths of glory at least lead to the Grave, but the paths of duty may not get you Anywhere.

The Unicorn in the Garden

ONCE upon a sunny morning a man who sat in a
breakfast nook looked up from his scrambled
eggs to see a white unicorn with a golden horn
quietly cropping the roses in the garden. The man
went up to the bedroom where his wife was still
asleep and woke her. "There's a unicorn in the garden," he said. "Eating roses." She opened one un-
friendly eye and looked at him. "The unicorn is a
mythical beast," she said, and turned her back on
him. The man walked slowly downstairs and out into
the garden. The unicorn was still there; he was now
browsing among the tulips. "Here, unicorn," said the
man, and he pulled up a lily and gave it to him. The
unicorn ate it gravely. With a high heart, because
there was a unicorn in his garden, the man went up-
stairs and roused his wife again. "The unicorn," he
said, "ate a lily." His wife sat up in bed and looked
at him, coldly. "You are a booby," she said, "and I
am going to have you put in the booby-hatch." The
man, who had never liked the words "booby" and
"booby-hatch," and who liked them even less on a
shining morning when there was a unicorn in the garden, thought for a moment. "We'll see about that,"
he said. He walked over to the door. "He has a golden
horn in the middle of his forehead," he told her.

Then he went back to the garden to watch the unicorn; but the unicorn had gone away. The man sat down among the roses and went to sleep.

As soon as the husband had gone out of the house, the wife got up and dressed as fast as she could. She was very excited and there was a gloat in her eye. She telephoned the police and she telephoned a psychiatrist; she told them to hurry to her house and bring a strait-jacket. When the police and the psychiatrist arrived they sat down in chairs and looked at her, with great interest. "My husband," she said, "saw a unicorn this morning." The police looked at the psychiatrist and the psychiatrist looked at the police. "He told me it ate a lily," she said. The psychiatrist looked at the police and the police looked at the psychiatrist. "He told me it had a golden horn in the middle of its forehead," she said. At a solemn signal from the psychiatrist, the police leaped from their chairs and seized the wife. They had a hard time subduing her, for she put up a terrific struggle, but they finally subdued her. Just as they got her into the strait-jacket, the husband came back into the house.

"Did you tell your wife you saw a unicorn?" asked the police. "Of course not," said the husband. "The unicorn is a mythical beast." "That's all I wanted to know," said the psychiatrist. "Take her away. I'm sorry, sir, but your wife is as crazy as a jay bird." So they took her away, cursing and screaming, and shut her up in an institution. The husband lived happily ever after.

Moral: Don't count your boobies until they are hatched.

The Rabbits Who
Caused All the Trouble

Within the memory of the youngest child there
was a family of rabbits who lived near a pack
of wolves. The wolves announced that they did not
like the way the rabbits were living. (The wolves
were crazy about the way they themselves were living,
because it was the only way to live.) One night
several wolves were killed in an earthquake and this
was blamed on the rabbits, for it is well known that
rabbits pound on the ground with their hind legs and
cause earthquakes. On another night one of the
wolves was killed by a bolt of lightning and this was
also blamed on the rabbits, for it is well known that
lettuce-eaters cause lightning. The wolves threatened
to civilize the rabbits if they didn't behave, and the
rabbits decided to run away to a desert island. But
the other animals, who lived at a great distance,
shamed them, saying, "You must stay where you are
and be brave. This is no world for escapists. If the
wolves attack you, we will come to your aid, in all
probability." So the rabbits continued to live near
the wolves and one day there was a terrible flood
which drowned a great many wolves. This was blamed
on the rabbits, for it is well known that carrot-nib-

blers with long ears cause floods. The wolves descended on the rabbits, for their own good, and imprisoned them in a dark cave, for their own protection.

When nothing was heard about the rabbits for some weeks, the other animals demanded to know what had happened to them. The wolves replied that the rabbits had been eaten and since they had been eaten the affair was a purely internal matter. But the other animals warned that they might possibly unite against the wolves unless some reason was given for the destruction of the rabbits. So the wolves gave them one. "They were trying to escape," said the wolves, "and, as you know, this is no world for escapists."

Moral: Run, don't walk, to the nearest desert island.

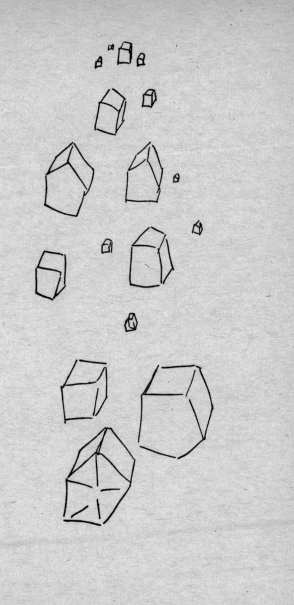

The Hen and the Heavens

ONCE upon a time a little red hen was picking up stones and worms and seeds in a barnyard when something fell on her head. "The heavens are falling down!" she shouted, and she began to run, still shouting, "The heavens are falling down!" All the hens that she met and all the roosters and turkeys and ducks laughed at her, smugly, the way you laugh at one who is terrified when you aren't. "What did you say?" they chortled. "The heavens are falling down!" cried the little red hen. Finally a very pompous rooster said to her, "Don't be silly, my dear, it was only a pea that fell on your head." And he laughed and laughed and everybody else except the little red hen laughed. Then suddenly with an awful roar great chunks of crystallized cloud and huge blocks of icy blue sky began to drop on everybody from above, and everybody was killed, the laughing rooster and the little red hen and everybody else in the barnyard, for the heavens actually *were* falling down.

Moral: It wouldn't surprise me a bit if they did.

Famous Poems
Illustrated

Excelsior

by HENRY WADSWORTH LONGFELLOW

The shades of night were falling fast,
As through an Alpine village passed
A youth, who bore, 'mid snow and ice,
A banner with the strange device—
                    Excelsior!

"Try not the pass," the old man said;
"Dark lowers the tempest overhead;
The roaring torrent is deep and wide!"
And loud that clarion voice replied,
               Excelsior!

"O stay," the maiden said, "and rest
Thy weary head upon this breast!"
A tear stood in his bright blue eye,
But still he answered, with a sigh,
        Excelsior!

"Beware the pine-tree's withered branch!
Beware the awful avalanche!"
This was the peasant's last good night:
A voice replied, far up the height,
        Excelsior!

At break of day, as heavenward
The pious monks of Saint Bernard
Uttered the oft-repeated prayer,
A voice cried through the startled air,
    Excelsior!

A traveller, by the faithful hound,
Half-buried in the snow was found,
Still grasping in his hand of ice
That banner with the strange device,
　　　　　Excelsior!

There in the twilight cold and gray,
Lifeless, but beautiful, he lay,
And from the sky, serene and far,
A voice fell, like a falling star—
　　　　　Excelsior!

The Sands o' Dee

by CHARLES KINGSLEY

"O Mary, go and call the cattle home,
    And call the cattle home,
    And call the cattle home,
  Across the sands o' Dee!"
The western wind was wild and dank wi' foam,
  And all alone went she.

The creeping tide came up along the sand,
    And o'er and o'er the sand,
    And round and round the sand,
  As far as eye could see;
The blinding mist came down and hid the land:
  And never home came she.

"O, is it weed, or fish, or floating hair—
    A tress o' golden hair,
      O' drownèd maiden's hair—
    Above the nets at sea?
Was never salmon yet that shone so fair
    Among the stakes on Dee."

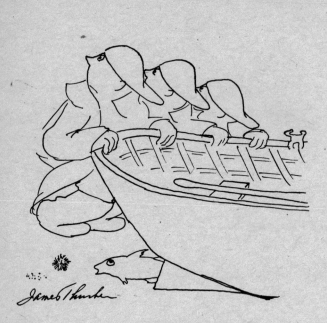

They rowed her in across the rolling foam,
    The cruel, crawling foam,
    The cruel, hungry foam,
  To her grave beside the sea;
But still the boatmen hear her call the cattle home
  Across the sands o' Dee.

Lochinvar

by SIR WALTER SCOTT

O, young Lochinvar is come out of the west,
Through all the wide Border his steed was the best;
And, save his good broadsword, he weapon had none,
He rode all unarmed, and he rode all alone.
So faithful in love, and so dauntless in war,
There never was knight like the young Lochinvar.

But, ere he alighted at Netherby gate,
The bride had consented, the gallant came late;
For a laggard in love, and a dastard in war,
Was to wed the fair Ellen of brave Lochinvar.
So boldly he entered the Netherby Hall,
Among bridesmen, and kinsmen, and brothers, and
    all.

Then spoke the bride's father, his hand on his sword
 (For the poor craven bridegroom said never a word),
"O come ye in peace here, or come ye in war,
Or to dance at our bridal, young Lord Lochinvar?"

"I long wooed your daughter, my suit you denied—
Love swells like the Solway, but ebbs like its tide—
And now I am come, with this lost love of mine,
To lead but one measure, drink one cup of wine,
There are maidens in Scotland more lovely by far,
That would gladly be bride to the young Lochinvar."

The bride kissed the goblet; the knight took it up,
He quaffed off the wine, and threw down the cup.
She looked down to blush, and she looked up to sigh,
With a smile on her lips, and a tear in her eye.
He took her soft hand, ere her mother could bar—
"Now tread we a measure," said young Lochinvar.

So stately his form, and so lovely her face,
That never a hall such a galliard did grace;
While her mother did fret, and her father did fume,
And the bridegroom stood dangling his bonnet and
    plume . . .

One touch to her hand, and one word in her ear,
When they reached the hall door, and the charger
stood near;
So light to the croupe the fair lady he swung,
So light to the saddle before her he sprung;
"She is won! we are gone! Over bank, bush, and
scaur;
They'll have fleet steeds that follow," quoth young
Lochinvar.

There was mounting 'mong Graemes of the Netherby
    clan;
Forsters, Fenwicks, and Musgraves, they rode and they
    ran;
There was racing and chasing on Cannobie Lee,
But the lost bride of Netherby ne'er did they see.
So daring in love, and so dauntless in war,
Have ye e'er heard of gallant like young Lochinvar?

Locksley Hall

by ALFRED, LORD TENNYSON

Comrades, leave me here a little, while as yet 'tis early
    morn;
Leave me here, and when you want me, sound upon
    the bugle horn.

'Tis the place, and all around it, as of old, the curlews
    call,
Dreary gleams about the moorland, flying over Locks-
    ley Hall.

In the spring a livelier iris changes on the burnished
   dove;
In the spring a young man's fancy lightly turns to
   thoughts of love.

O my cousin, shallow-hearted! O, my Amy, mine no
   more!
O the dreary, dreary moorland! O the barren, barren
   shore!

Is it well to wish thee happy?—having known me; to
  decline
On a range of lower feelings and a narrower heart
  than mine!

As the husband is, the wife is; thou art mated with a
  clown,
And the grossness of his nature will have weight to
  drag thee down.

Like a dog, he hunts in dreams; and thou art staring
    at the wall,
Where the dying night-lamp flickers, and the shadows
    rise and fall.

Then a hand shall pass before thee, pointing to his
    drunken sleep,
To thy widowed marriage-pillows, to the tears that
    thou wilt weep.

Hark! my merry comrades call me, sounding on the
    bugle-horn,—
They to whom my foolish passion were a target for
    their scorn.

. . . I will take some savage woman, she shall rear my
dusky race.

Iron-jointed, supple-sinewed, they shall dive, and they
shall run,
Catch the wild goat by the hair, and hurl their lances
in the sun.

Fool, again the dream, the fancy! but I *know* my
words are wild . . .

O, I see the crescent promise of my spirit hath not set;
Ancient founts of inspiration well through all my
    fancy yet.

. . . a long farewell to Locksley Hall!
Now for me the woods may wither, now for me the
    roof-tree fall.

Comes a vapor from the margin, blackening over
    heath and holt,
Cramming all the blast before it, in its breast a thun-
    derbolt.

Let it fall on Locksley Hall, with rain or hail, or fire
    or snow;
For the mighty wind arises, roaring seaward, and I go.

"Oh When I Was . . ."[1]

by A. E. HOUSMAN

Oh when I was in love with you,
Then I was clean and brave,
And miles around the wonder grew
How well did I behave.

[1] FROM A SHROPSHIRE LAD, *by A. E. Housman, by permission of Henry Holt & Company.*

And now the fancy passes by,
And nothing will remain,
And miles around they'll say that I
Am quite myself again.

Curfew Must Not Ring To-Night

by ROSE HARTWICK THORPE

"Sexton," Bessie's white lips faltered, pointing to the
    prison old,
With its turrets tall and gloomy, with its walls dark,
    damp, and cold,
"I've a lover in that prison, doomed this very night
    to die,
At the ringing of the Curfew, and no earthly help is
    nigh;
Cromwell will not come till sunset," and her lips grew
    strangely white
As she breathed the husky whisper:—
                 "Curfew must not ring to-night."

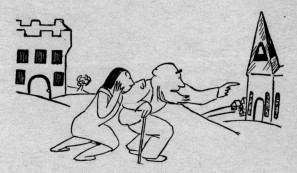

"Bessie," calmly spoke the sexton—every word pierced
    her young heart
Like the piercing of an arrow, like a deadly poisoned
    dart—
"Long, long years I've rung the Curfew from that
    gloomy, shadowed tower;
Every evening, just at sunset, it has told the twilight
    hour;
I have done my duty ever, tried to do it just and right,
Now I'm old I will not falter—
                    Curfew, it must ring to-night."

With quick step she bounded forward, sprang within
the old church door,
Left the old man threading slowly paths so oft he'd
trod before;
Not one moment paused the maiden, but with eye
and cheek aglow
Mounted up the gloomy tower, where the bell swung
to and fro:
As she climbed the dusty ladder, on which fell no ray
of light,
Up and up—her white lips saying:—
"Curfew must not ring to-night."

She has reached the topmost ladder; o'er her hangs
    the great dark bell;
Awful is the gloom beneath her, like the pathway
    down to hell.
Lo, the ponderous tongue is swinging—'tis the hour of
    Curfew now,
And the sight has chilled her bosom, stopped her
    breath, and paled her brow.
Shall she let it ring? No, never! flash her eyes with
    sudden light,
As she springs and grasps it firmly—
                "Curfew shall not ring to-night!"

Out she swung—far out; the city seemed a speck of
    light below,
There 'twixt heaven and earth suspended as the bell
    swung to and fro,
And the sexton at the bell rope, old and deaf, heard
    not the bell,
Sadly thought, "That twilight Curfew rang young
    Basil's funeral knell."
Still the maiden clung more firmly and with trem-
    bling lips so white,
Said to hush her heart's wild throbbing:—
                    "Curfew shall not ring to-night!"

O'er the distant hills came Cromwell; Bessie sees him,
and her brow,
Lately white with fear and anguish, has no anxious
traces now.
At his feet she tells her story, shows her hands all
bruised and torn;
And her face so sweet and pleading, yet with sor-
row pale and worn,
Touched his heart with sudden pity, lit his eyes with
misty light:
"Go! your lover lives," said Cromwell,
"Curfew shall not ring to-night."

Wide they flung the massive portal; led the prisoner
    forth to die—
All his bright young life before him. 'Neath the dark-
    ening English sky
Bessie comes with flying footsteps, eyes aglow with
    love-light sweet;
Kneeling on the turf beside him, lays his pardon at
    his feet.
In his brave, strong arms he clasped her, kissed the
    face upturned and white,
Whispered, "Darling, you have saved me—
                  "Curfew will not ring to-night!"

Barbara Frietchie

by JOHN GREENLEAF WHITTIER

On that pleasant morn of the early fall
When Lee marched over the mountain wall;

Over the mountains winding down,
Horse and foot, into Frederick town,

Forty flags with their silver stars,
Forty flags with their crimson bars,

Flapped in the morning wind . . .

[135]

. . . the sun
Of noon looked down, and saw not one.

Up rose old Barbara Frietchie then,
Bowed with her fourscore years and ten;

Bravest of all in Frederick town,
She took up the flag the men hauled down;

In her attic window the staff she set,
To show that one heart was loyal yet.

Up the street came the rebel tread,
Stonewall Jackson riding ahead.

Under his slouched hat left and right
He glanced; the old flag met his sight.

"Halt!"—the dust-brown ranks stood fast;
"Fire!"—out blazed the rifle-blast.

It shivered the window, pane and sash;
It rent the banner with seam and gash.

Quick, as it fell, from the broken staff
Dame Barbara snatched the silken scarf.

She leaned far out on the window-sill,
And shook it forth with a royal will.

"Shoot, if you must, this old gray head,
But spare your country's flag," she said.

A shade of sadness, a blush of shame,
Over the face of the leader came;

The nobler nature within him stirred
To life at that woman's deed and word;

"Who touches a hair of yon gray head
Dies like a dog! March on!" he said.

All day long through Frederick street
Sounded the tread of marching feet:

All day long that free flag tossed
Over the heads of the rebel host.

Ever its torn folds rose and fell
On the loyal winds that loved it well;

And through the hill-gaps sunset light
Shone over it with a warm good-night . . .

The Glove and the Lions

by LEIGH HUNT

King Francis was a hearty king, and loved a royal
    sport,
And one day, as his lions fought, sat looking at the
    court.
The nobles filled the benches, and the ladies in their
    pride,
And 'mongst them sat the Count de Lorge, with one
    for whom he sighed:
And truly 'twas a gallant thing to see that crowning
    show,
Valor and love, and a king above, and the royal beasts
    below.

Ramped and roared the lions, with horrid laughing
    jaws;
They bit, they glared, gave blows like beams, a wind
    went with their paws;
With wallowing might and stifled roar they rolled on
    one another,
Till all the pit with sand and mane was in a thun-
    derous smother.

The bloody foam above the bars came whisking
    through the air;
Said Francis then, "Faith, gentlemen, we're better
    here than there."

De Lorge's love o'erheard the King, a beauteous lively
   dame,
With smiling lips and sharp bright eyes, which always
   seemed the same;
She thought, "The Count, my lover, is brave as brave
   can be;
He surely would do wondrous things to show his love
   of me;
King, ladies, lovers, all look on; the occasion is divine;
I'll drop my glove, to prove his love; great glory will
   be mine."
She dropped her glove, to prove his love, then looked
   at him and smiled;

He bowed, and in a moment leaped among the lions
    wild;

The leap was quick, return was quick, he has regained
    his place,
Then threw the glove, but not with love, right in the
    lady's face.
"By Heaven," said Francis, "rightly done!" and he
    rose from where he sat;
"No love," quoth he, "but vanity, sets love a task like
    that."

Ben Bolt

by THOMAS DUNN ENGLISH

Don't you remember sweet Alice, Ben Bolt—
  Sweet Alice whose hair was so brown,
Who wept with delight when you gave her a smile,

And trembled with fear at your frown?

In the old churchyard in the valley, Ben Bolt,
   In a corner obscure and alone,
  They have fitted a slab of the granite so gray
   And Alice lies under the stone.

And don't you remember the school, Ben Bolt,
    With the master so cruel and grim,
And the shaded nook in the running brook
    Where the children went to swim?

Grass grows on the master's grave, Ben Bolt,
  The spring of the brook is dry,

And of all the boys who were schoolmates then
  There are only you and I.